Great Women in Bahamian History

DEANNE HANNA-EWERS
Author

KELLI HICKSON
Editor

LAVAUGHN SANDS
Assistant Editor

AuthorHouse™
1663 Liberty Drive
Bloomington, IN 47403
www.authorhouse.com
Phone: 1-800-839-8640

Published by AuthorHouse
12/27/2012
ISBN: 978-1-4520-5398-1 (sc)
ISBN: 978-1-4772-9249-5 (e)

Deanne Hanna-Ewers
Author

Kelli Hickson
Editor

LaVaughn Sands
Assistant Editor

Acknowledgements

I would like to thank the following individuals for their efforts in assisting me with this project:

Chris Bain
The Nassau Tribune,
NP, Bahamas

Anastasia Forbes
The Bahamian Collection of
The College of the Bahamas

Corporal Hanna
The Royal Bahamas Police Force,
Public Relations Department

Patrick Hanna
Professional Photographer-
Bahamas Information Services

Tarara Johnson
Teacher; Riviera Beach, Florida

LaVaughn Sands
Teacher; C. C. Sweeting Senior
High School, Nassau, NP Bahamas

Dr. Yvette Stuart
Nassau, NP, Bahamas

Brent Stubbs
Senior Sports Reporter-
The Tribune, Nassau, NP Bahamas

My apologies are extended to other notable great women who were not mentioned in this edition.

A Tribute
To the Women of Penny Savings Sub Division off Soldier Road West

Through My Corner

Through my corner are the most beautiful women the world has ever seen

They are sincere, diligent and honest - women who have kept their surroundings clean

They have produced Technicians, a Pilot, a Pharmacist, an Engineer and Teachers too; a

Permanent Secretary, Entrepreneurs, Photographers and Civil Servants

They bake cakes and cook the best meals

They are there to comfort each other when bereaved

They have prayed together and laughed together and have had many chats...

And throughout the years that I have known them, they have never had a spat!

Through my corner are the most beautiful women the world has ever seen

They are women of faith, women of courage and women of strength

These are women who are worthy of high esteem:

Blanche Campbell

Shirley Cartwright

Lorraine Charlton

Cynthia Duncombe

Drucilla Ferguson

Leanzar Mae Tinker-Hanna "my mother"

Alberta Miller

Louise Rolle (deceased)

Dame Justice Joan Sawyer

Prefix

This book celebrates women of the Bahamas. To every woman born on the Bahamian soil this book shows what can be achieved through hard work and determination. This book showcases the strength and vitality of Bahamian Women and it proves that there are no boundaries to what women are capable of attaining.

This is a special book not just because it features women who have made great strides and contributions to the Bahamian society, but because it features women born in the Bahamas exclusively.

This is an authentic Bahamian history book that will prove to be timeless, as well as a great source of information for the next generation. This is also a reference book that is easy to read and comprehend. *Great Women in Bahamian History* is a book of inspiration, courage and motivation. Most importantly, this is also a book that features women who were the *first* to break barriers in areas that were once male dominated.

Contents

1 BUSINESS   1

2 COMMUNICATIONS 11

3 EDUCATION   17

4 GOVERNMENT   25

5 LAW/LAW ENFORCEMENT 41

6 MEDICINE/ HEALTH   49

7 MUSIC   59

Contents cont'd

8   POLITICS   63

9   RELIGION   77

10 SPORTS   83

OTHER NOTABLE
WOMEN IN BAHAMIAN
HISTORY   95

ABOUT THE AUTHOR   103

Foreword

This book is a welcome edition to the documented research on women in the Bahamas. It will prove to be very helpful to those not only interested in women's affairs but it will also benefit those involved with other topics as well.

It is an easy read and provides a starting point for those interested in further academic research.

I understand that a second work in this series is forthcoming. I look forward to its release.

Yvette Stuart Ph. D.
Mass *Communications*
Nassau, NP Bahamas

CHAPTER 1
BUSINESS

Pauline Allen-Dean

D ean was the first Bahamian woman manager of a commercial bank in The Bahamas, and the first Bahamian woman to serve as managing director of a commercial bank. Dean was also the first Bahamian woman to be elected a fellow of Chartered Institute of Bankers in 1983. Dean completed a Diploma in Banking from the Institute of Bankers, London (1973).

Paula Allen-Dean was elected president of The Bahamas Institute of Bankers in 1998 and was the past President of the Zonta Club of Nassau. Dean also held the position of Deputy President of the Bahamas Red Cross Society. After completing

(continued on page 2)

her term as Deputy President, Dean now serves as an active volunteer of the Bahamas Red Cross, and holds the position of Raffle Committee Chairperson.

As an activist, Dean was the founding president of the Consumer Protection Association and the Women Against Rape (WAR) Association. Dean is a charter member of the Business and Professional Women's Association of the Bahamas, and has been successful in an effort to ensure that women be placed on The Bahamas Jurors' List. Dean is a former Nassau Guardian columnist, who wrote articles under the heading, *"One Woman's Point of View."* Her latest project has been launching a 200 Home Community Development with her brother, former Cabinet Minister Algernon Allen. This community is located in 'Coral Breeze Estates' which is a 50 acre private home development in the Coral Harbor area.

Theresa Mortimer

I n 2002, Theresa Mortimer made Bahamian history by being elected the first president and first Bahamian woman president of the Bahamas Financial Services Union (BFSU). Mortimer graduated from Government High School in 1979. After high school, she pursued a degree in banking at the College of The Bahamas. Her career in the financial industry commenced in 1982 at First Caribbean International, formerly Barclays Bank PLC. After 26 years of service, she took an early retirement in December 2007.

As a trade unionist, Mortimer presently serves as the third Vice President of The National Congress of Trade Union of The Bahamas (NCTU). In addition, she is a titular for Union

(continued on page 4)

Network International Financial Sector, (UNI). Mortimer believes that the strength of the union lies within its membership. Therefore under Mortimer's leadership, their goal is to develop a plan of action to encourage all financial institutes to become members of BFSU.

Mortimer is the daughter of Harry Sands (deceased) and Dorothy Sands. She is married to Renbert Mortimer Sr. (deceased), and the couple has two children, Renbert Jr. and Rena. Motimer worships at a Baptist church.

Judy V. C. Munroe

Munroe is well known as the first Bahamian woman to become president of The Bahamas Chamber of Commerce, a position she held from 1979-1982. Munroe was also the first female Chairman of the Ecumenical Co-operative Society, in the Netherlands and Antilles.

In 1980, Munroe was named *"Woman of the Year"* and in 1987, she was named *"Person of the Year"*. In 2004, Munroe was awarded an Officer of the Order of the British Empire {OBE} by Her Majesty Queen Elizabeth II.

Munroe served as Chief Executive Officer and President of the Caribbean Bottling Company, Bahamas Limited. Munroe

(continued on page 6)

also served as the Charter President of the Zonta Club of Nassau, as well as chairperson of the Salvation Army Advisory Board. Munroe is a chairperson of the National Women's Advisory Council and the Bahamian Women's Forum respectively. Munroe graduated from Government High School in 1957, and later earned an MBA from the University of Miami.

Winifred Russell

ussell is the first Bahamian woman to hold fellowships in both General and Life Insurances (the highest degrees within the insurance business). For twenty-six years Russell has been in the insurance business where she is a member of the Fellow of the Life Management Institute (FLMI) and a Fellow of the Insurance Institute of Canada (FIIC). Russell has been instrumental in creating SHAPE, the first Bahamian Managed Care Health Insurance program.

In addition, Russell has served as president of the Bahamas Netball Association for some fourteen years and has been a member of the Bahamas Sports Council from its inception. In

(continued on page 8)

1995, Russell was honored by "Sports Magazine" and inducted into the "Hall of Fame" for her contributions to sports. Russell is a member of the Zonta Club of Nassau.

In recent times, Russell has acquired the prestigious achievement of Legal Education Certificate (LEC) from the Eugene Dupuch Law School in 2008. She has also attained the status of Attorney At Law with a Bachelor of Laws Degree (LLB) from the University of the West Indies/College of the Bahamas in 2008. Russell is a widow with two biological sons, as well as adopted children.

Manita Wisdom

I n 1987 Wisdom became the first Bahamian woman and first black woman to be inducted into the American list of Floral Designers. Wisdom is also the only Bahamian woman with the (AIFD) American Institute of Floral Designers Designation.

In 1999-2000, Wisdom was featured in the SAF (Society of American Florist) directory. Wisdom was also inducted into the Canadian Floral Design in 1992. Wisdom is a 1989 member of the Society of American Florist and has prepared flowers for Queen Elizabeth II, Queen of England and the former Prime Minister of India. In 1987, Wisdom's floral work was featured in numerous international magazines and her worked was presented for the Black Florist Association of America. Wisdom

(continued on page 10)

has had the opportunity to present flowers at the Institute of Floral Design Symposium in Orlando, Florida. Wisdom presently owns and operates a state of the art Floral store located on West Bay Street, Nassau, N.P. the Bahamas. Wisdom is married to the Honourable Neville Wisdom (former Minister of Youth and Arts, Culture & Housing) and the couple has one son, Donovan.

CHAPTER 2
COMMUNICATIONS

Eileen Dupuch Carron

I n 1993, Carron became the first Bahamian woman to purchase and launch a radio station (100 JAMZ) in the Bahamas, as well as in the Caribbean. Carron was also the first Bahamian woman to have graduated with a Master's degree in Communications from Columbia School of Journalism in New York. Moreover, Carron was also the first to have her editorials read into the U.S. Senate Record. In addition, she was the first trained female member of the Nassau Flying Club.

In 1972, Carron became the second Bahamian woman editor of one of the local newspapers, The Tribune, the newspaper

(continued on page 12)

founded by her grandfather, Leon Dupuch. In 1962, Carron became the second Bahamian woman to be called to The Bahamas Bar. Carron was Barrister-at-Law of Lincoln's Inn and was called to the English Bar in that same year. *"For services to the growth and development of the Bahamas"* Carron was named a Companion of the Order of St Michael and St George (CMG) in June of 2000.

Carron was married to the former managing editor of the Tribune, the late Roger Carron originally of Eastbourne, Sussex, England. The couple was married for 46 years and has one son.

Sandra J. Knowles

O n Friday, January 8th, 1993 the announcement was made that Sandra J. Knowles was to become the first Bahamian woman to head ZNS Radio and Television stations. She held this position from 1993-1997. Knowles was responsible for the first major technological upgrade of the television facilities since its inception, emphasizing strong focus on local programming in television and radio.

Knowles was a former educator at The Government High School where she headed the History Department. Later, she worked as an Assistant Manager of the Investment Departments of Coutts and Company. A graduate of the University of Miami, Knowles was trained at the Canadian Broadcasting Corporation

(continued on page 14)

in Toronto before taking on the position as General Manager of ZNS.

Furthermore, from 1997 to 2002, Ms. Knowles became the first female Inspector and Executive Director of the Securities Commission of The Bahamas. She was instrumental in formulating policies for the promotion of an efficient and knowledgeable regulatory environment.

Mary Moseley (deceased)

A fter the death of her father in 1904, Moseley took on the position of the first woman editor and manager of a local newspaper, *The Nassau Guardian*. In 1926, Moseley wrote the first edition of The Bahamas Handbook. Furthermore, she became a Bahamian historian and was nominated as a trustee for the Nassau Public Library and Museum. Later, Moseley became Chairperson of the Trusteeship Committee.

In 1917 Moseley contributed in the war. After that, she formed the Ladies Committee of the West Indian Contingent. She was given the member of the British Empire award by King George V. Moseley was the granddaughter of the founder and first editor of *The Nassau Guardian*. She was born in 1878 and died in 1960.

Deanne Hanna-Ewers

CHAPTER 3
EDUCATION

Dr. Keva Marie Bethel (deceased)

I n 1982, Bethel made history by becoming the first Bahamian woman principal of The College of the Bahamas (COB). Thirteen years later in 1995, Bethel was appointed president of the autonomous College of the Bahamas until her retirement in 1998. While at COB, Bethel helped establish private scholarships for deserving Bahamian students. She was also involved in enabling COB to move from an Associate's Degree college to a Baccalaureate Degree level college.

In 1996, Bethel became the recipient of the Paul Harris Award from the South East Rotary Club. Bethel also received

(continued on page 18)

17

the International Woman's Forum Award in 1994. She became a companion of the Order of St. Michael and St. George (CMG) in 1995. Bethel, former chairperson for the National Advisory Council for Education and board member of FINCO, had other outstanding achievements such as having received the Business Woman's Award of 1982 from the Business and Professional Women's Association of The Bahamas. Bethel also received the Chamber of Commerce Award for Government in 1986.

Dr. Desiree Cox

In 1986 Cox made history by becoming the first Bahamian woman and the first woman in the Caribbean to receive the Rhodes Scholarship. This two year scholarship was created by "Cecil Rhodes in 1902 to recruit and bring top men from several nations to Oxford to be initiated into the Illuminati and to learn about how to bring in a One-World-Government" that would promote unity among English-speaking nations.(www.greatdreams.com/Fhodes-Scholars.htm)

First, Cox studied science at McGill University (Montreal, Canada) where she specialized in Quantum chemistry, receiving a BSc. (Hon) in Chemistry in 1986. In 1987 Cox went to Oxford University where she studied medicine as a Rhodes Scholar.

(continued on page 20)

After qualifying as a medical doctor she obtained a Master of Philosophy (MPhil) and a PhD in History of Medicine from the University at Cambridge. In 2004, Cox was described as a *'Renaissance Woman'* by the British Medical Journal (BMJ). Cox worked as a medical doctor in London for a number of years before returning to the Bahamas where she served as a co-founder, consultant and advisor to the Prime Minister of the Bahamas in the area of Human Development and Urban Renewal Initiative between 2004 and 2007.

In 2005, Cox founded Soul Imagination. Cox now spends her time bringing together art and live music performances in the public spaces of hospitals to transform depressing spaces into healing ones. Cox is an international key-note speaker, as well as an Associate Lecturer at the University of the West Indies in Ethics and Humanities.

Since 2004, Cox has lived in the Bahamas. She divides her time between Nassau (Bahamas) and the UK (her home for over

(continued on page 21)

16 years). She has held a number of art exhibitions in The Bahamas and has released 2 Jazz CD's in 2005 and 2007. Her first work of fiction *'Edge of the Sea'* was published in 2008. (www.soulimagination.com)

Cox is presently focusing exclusively on her creative talents as a full-time visionary artist/painter, writer, and as an independent consultant in Human Development and social entrepreneurship.

Anatol Rodgers (deceased)

Anatol Rogers was the first Bahamian woman principal of The Government High School. She held this position from 1971-1975. Rodgers began her teaching career at Western Senior School. She taught there for a year before being appointed as Assistant Mistress at Government High School.

Rodgers is one of the original members of the Board of Management of the Ranfurly Home for Children. She also served as a member of the Juvenile Court and president of the Carver Garden Club. Rodgers was educated at Government High School and later pursued degrees at Spelman College and Atlanta University in Atlanta, Georgia, USA. Rodgers is the

(continued on page 23)

daughter of the great educator, C. H. Reeves. In 2008, the Bahamas government named a south-western high school in her honor.

Deanne Hanna-Ewers

CHAPTER 4
GOVERNMENT

Patricia E. Bethel

Bethel is known as the first Bahamian woman technical officer to have reached the level of Assistant Director in the Department of Fisheries. She first began her employment as a Trainee Executive Officer in the Ministry of Foreign Affairs and later transferred to the Ministry of Fisheries where she worked for eighteen years. Bethel is presently implementing a system that would ensure the safety of the seafood produced for domestic and international consumption.

Bethel is the President of Kruger Plastics, a unique Bahamian company that manufactures plastic bags.

Juliette Barnwell

Barnwell is known as the first Bahamian woman to be elected Chairperson to an Administrative Board of a local Public school, namely C. R. Walker Secondary School; the school named after her father.

Barnwell was also the first Bahamian woman director and president of The Bahamas Cooperative League. She was also the Chairman of the Cooperative Advisory Committee. Barnwell was the past recipient of the Bahamahost award, a Bahamahost Lecturer, Justice of the Peace and a Lay Magistrate.

Barnwell was awarded the Silver Jubilee Award for her work in cooperative development. She was also awarded the honor of Lieutenant of the Royal Victorian Order (RVO) during the

(continued on page 27)

25th anniversary of her Majesty the Queen. Barnwell was the first chairperson of the Limited Bahamas Cooperative League. Barnwell is the mother of three children, one of whom is deceased.

Dame Ivy Dumont

On January 1st, 2002, Dame Dumont became the first Bahamian woman to be appointed to the position of Governor-General of The Commonwealth of The Bahamas. Dame Ivy assumed office of Acting Governor-General in November 13th 2001.

Dumont started her career in the Department of Education from 1948-1975 first as a student teacher. She then moved up the ranks to become Director of Education. Dumont also served as Deputy Permanent Secretary in the Ministry of Works and Utilities from 1975-1978. Under the Free National Movement Party, Dumont was appointed to the Senate and sworn in as Minister of Health and Environment on August 24, 1992. On

(continued on page 29)

January 9, 1995 Dumont was appointed Minister of Education and Training. She was re-appointed to this post on March 18, 1997 and later retired in January 2001.

Dame Ivy graduated from the Government High School in 1948. In 1951, she furthered her studies at The Bahamas Teachers' Training College and in 1970 she graduated from the University of Miami. She also graduated from Nova Southeastern University in 1978. Dame Ivy most recent achievement is her memoir entitled, *Rose's to Mount Fitzwilliam*.

Dame Ivy is married to Reginald Dean Dumont, a retired Police Inspector and Prices Control Inspector. The couple has two children.

Claire L. Hepburn

Claire L. Hepburn is known as the first Bahamian woman to hold the position of Chairperson of The Gaming Board of the Commonwealth of the Bahamas. She is also the first Bahamian woman to hold the position of Chairperson of the Broadcasting Corporation of the Bahamas from 1992-1994.

Hepburn is the former vice-principal of The College of the Bahamas and the past president of the Zonta Club of Nassau. Hepburn is a lawyer who was admitted to the Bahamas Bar in 1985. Having served under articles of clerkship, Mrs. Hepburn was admitted as Counsel and Attorney of the Supreme Court of the Bahamas on September 27, 1985 and entered the firm of

(continued on page 31)

Graham, Thompson & Co. She was admitted to partnership in May 1990.

After being appointed a Senator on May 4, 2007, Mrs. Hepburn served as Attorney General and Minister of Legal Affairs from that date until July 7, 2008.

His Excellency, the Governor-General, on the advice of the Judicial and Legal Service Commission, appointed Mrs. Claire Hepburn as a Justice of the Supreme Court, She assumed office on October 1, 2008.

Hepburn was educated at Government High School, and at the University of the West Indies, Jamaica. There, she was awarded a Bachelor of Arts degree in History (Special Honors) in August of 1969 and a Diploma in Education the following year. She was awarded a Master of Education degree from the University of Miami in May of 1977.

Mrs. Hepburn is a Director of the Tara Xavier Hepburn Foundation and one of the coordinators of the T.A.R.A. Project,

(continued on page 32)

which was launched by the Foundation on October 13th, 2007. The program is designed to enrich the lives of young people between the ages of 9 and 18 years old by helping them to become responsible and productive citizens.

Hepburn is an Anglican. She is married to Livingston Hepburn and they are parents of two children, Ian Andre Hepburn and a daughter, Tara Xavier Hepburn (now deceased).

Constance McDonald

In 1997, McDonald became the first Bahamian woman appointed Acting Vice-President of the Bahamas Industrial Tribunal. In 1994, McDonald opened her own firm, McDonald and Co. in Freeport, GrandBahama. Since 1997, McDonald has served as president of the Grand Bahamas Chamber of Commerce.

McDonald is a past president of the Zonta Club in Freeport and a past president of the Guild of Graduates from the University of the West Indies. McDonald is also a former Acting Magistrate.

Margaret McDonald

In 1986, Margaret McDonald became the first Bahamian woman to be appointed Ambassador to the United States. McDonald was also named the first Bahamian woman to be appointed secretary to the Cabinet in 1982.

McDonald was a longtime teacher and civil servant. She also served as secretary to the Cabinet from November 1985-July 1986. A year earlier in 1985, Queen Elizabeth made McDonald Commander of the Royal Victorian Order and in 1980 she was made Commander of the British Empire as a part of the Queen's New Years' Honors List. McDonald graduated from the University of Pittsburgh's School of Public & International Affairs. McDonald has two children.

Melanie Roach

In 2001, Melanie Roach was appointed the first Bahamian woman Director of Public Works. In 1996, Roach was promoted to Deputy Director of Public Works and was responsible for the Building Surveys Section, the Mechanical and Electrical Engineering Section, Buildings Control, Subdivisions Section, and the General Services Division.

From 1990 to 1992, Roach served as Civil Works Coordinator and from 1993 to 1996 she served as the Buildings Control Officer responsible for day-to-day administration of the Buildings Control Section. Furthermore, from 1986 to 1987, Roach served as the Assistant Engineer for the Family Island

(continued on page 36)

section of the Ministry where she was responsible for the design of docks and the supervision of road and dock construction contracts. Moreover, from 1982 to 1985, Roach was an assistant engineer at the Ministry of Public Works.

Dr. Gail Saunders

D
r. Gail Saunders is known as the first Bahamian woman Archivist. Saunders gained this title in 1971 and was appointed as Chief Archivist in 1980. In 1983, she was appointed Director of the Department of the Archives, and the Ministry of Education. For more than 30 years, Dr. Saunders has been preserving the culture, history and heritage of The Bahamas. Effective July 2009, Dr. Gail Saunders was appointed Director-General of Heritage.

Saunders is the author of several books: *Bahamian Loyalist and Their Slaves*, London, 1983; *The Bahamas: A Family of Islands* London, 1988; *Slavery in The Bahamas* 1648-1838, Nassau, 1985. Saunders has also co-authored *Historic Nassau*,

(continued on page 38)

London, 1979 with Donald Cartwright, as well as *Guide to the Records of The Bahamas*, Nassau, 1973 with E.A. Carson.

Dr. Saunders was awarded an Honorary Doctorate of Laws degree from the Mona Campus of the University of the West Indies in Jamaica, a crowning achievement in her career. Saunders was born in Nassau on March 10, 1944, to Basil and Audrey North. She received her early education at Queens' College and graduated in 1966 with an honors degree in History from the University of Newcastle-Upon-Tyne, England, United Kingdom.

Vernice Walkine

W alkine is the first Bahamian woman Director
General of the Bahamas Ministry of Tourism;
a high-ranking position. Her influence over the
years has made her a force in shaping government and private
policy on the development of the tourist industry in the
Bahamas. In 2002, she was identified by *Travel Agent
Magazine* as one of the 100 most influential women in tourism
and travel in the world.

Walkine is a high profile and influential member of
Bahamian society and member of the College of The Bahamas
Alumnae. Vernice Walkine, has been appointed to The College
Council, the body charged with the general responsibility for

(continued on page 40)

the educational policy and administration of The College of The Bahamas.   Walkine was inducted into the <u>College of the Bahamas 'Alumni Association Hall of Fame</u> in 2005. Walkine was among one of the first groups of students to graduate from the new College of The Bahamas in 1977.

CHAPTER 5
LAW/LAW ENFORCEMENT

Supreme Court Senior Justice Anita Allen

Allen is known as the first Bahamian woman principal Legal Draftsman. In 1996, she became the second Bahamian woman appointed to the Supreme Court of the Bahamas. In 2007 Senior Justice Anita Allen was sworn in as Acting Chief Justice of the Supreme Court by Governor-General His Excellency the Hon. Arthur D. Hanna at Government House, Nassau Bahamas.

Keisa Arthur

On June 16, 2003, Arthur along with four other women joined The Royal Bahamas Police Force "C" Fire Squad. While working in the Fire Department, Arthur was among the first Bahamian women licensed to drive a fire truck along with WPC 278 Kenya Fowler. As a child, Arthur was always amazed by fires and fire trucks. After witnessing several house fires and feeling helpless to assist in some way, Arthur vowed that when she grew up that she would become a firefighter so that she could help save lives and properties.

Arthur is a graduate of the Government High School where she was a flagette in the school's initial marching band. Two of her favorite political figures are Nelson Mandela and Barack Obama.

Dame Joan Augusta Sawyer

On September 4, 2001, Dame Sawyer became the first Bahamian woman President of the Appeals Court. Five years earlier, Sawyer made history as she was sworn in as the first Bahamian woman Chief Justice on October 26, 1996. Sawyer is the third Bahamian Chief Justice in the Bahamas since the country's independence in 1973. She was also the first Bahamian woman Supreme Court Judge.

On July 19,1973 Dame Joan Sawyer was called to the English Bar, and in September of the same year she was called to the Bahamas Bar. Dame Sawyer served as acting Supreme Court judge from August to November of 1987, and was appointed to the position of Justice of the Supreme Court May 6, 1988. In addition, in1996 Queen Elizabeth made Sawyer a Dame Commanderof the Most Excellent Order of the British Empire.

 *Allerdyce Strachan*

In September 1996 Strachan became the first Bahamian Woman Superintendent in the Royal Bahamas Police Force. In 1988 Strachan was also the first woman to become a Gazetted Senior Police Officer. She was responsible for women police and personnel.

Strachan first joined the Force in 1965 when the Force opened its doors to women. Strachan moved from the rank of Corporal to Sergeant, then Inspector and Chief Inspector until she was promoted to Assistant Superintendent.

The First Bahamian Women Enlisted in the Royal Bahamas Police Force

T he presence of women in the Bahamas Police Force became more recognized in the 1960's. It all started with an Act giving women the right to vote and sit in the Legislature. This first opportunity for women to vote was held in the 1962 November elections. Two years later in 1964, women were allowed to join the Royal Bahamas Police Force and 122 women applied to become police officers.

In November 23, 1964 (6) six females began training under the supervision of Sergeant 286 Audrey Weigh: Anita Bethel, Theresa Baker, Norma Clarke, Alsaida McFall, Hildred McClain and Esther Stubbs.

However, before the initial training of policewomen, a matron was used to assist in the arrest of women. *"It is not*

(continued on page 46)

known who the first Matron of the Police Force was. However,

record dating as far back as December 1912; indicated that

sleeping quarters were made available for her at the Central

Police Station. From the 1930s through the 1940s and 1950s,

Mrs. Clothida Blackman served as Matron. She was a qualified

nurse and wife of former Sergeant 67 Blackman."

It should be noted that women officers received the same training as their male counterparts. Moreover, since the first squad of females, women have moved into many areas in the Force. Special mention is given to those who were the first in their area:

- On June 27, 1979 Dorothy Davis was the first Bahamian woman to attain the rank of Inspector. She also worked as a prosecutor.

- In 1984, WPC 1572 Pauline Ferguson was the first female to become a dog handler.

(continued on page 47)

- On January 9, 1985 WPC 1632 Killy Heastie was the first female attached to the Airwing Section.

- On October 1, 1987 Inspector Denise Tynes was the first female to enter at this rank in the Force. She joined the staff of the Forensic Science Laboratory.

- WPC 976 Ruby Collie-Saunders was the first woman motorcyclist.

- The First Woman Police Fingerprint Expert and Photographer was Assistant Superintendent Delmeta Turnquest. Turnquest studied at Durham Constabulary in Durham, England in 1970.

Deanne Hanna-Ewers

CHAPTER 6
MEDICINE/HEALTH

Dr. Vernell Theresa Allen G
W

Allen is known as the first Bahamian woman Chief Medical Officer. She was one of the first Bahamian women to enter the field of Medicine in the Bahamas. In 1978 she was appointed Deputy Chief Medical Officer and assumed the post of CMO in 1981. While in office, Allen made changes in the areas of community clinics, adolescent, children school services and helped to improve public health services throughout the Bahamas.

Hilda V. Bowen (deceased)

Bowen attended school in the United Kingdom from 1946 to 1953, qualifying with a degree in Nursing and Midwifery with a specialization in Ophthalmology.

She was appointed the first Bahamian matron of the hospital in 1962, and after three years she was appointed Chief Nursing Officer in the Ministry of Health. In that capacity, she was in charge of coordinating all of the nursing services in The Bahamas, including the Family Island. In this post, she aided the development of the Nursing Council, the Statutory Body governing nursing practice in the country.

(continued on page 51)

Bowen's most distinguished accomplishment was in having nursing recognised as a profession. She was most influential in developing modern nursing in the Bahamas and in 1969 was awarded the MBE for her contribution to the Nursing Service and Nursing Education in the Bahamas. She was also involved in the Women's suffrage movement, the Red Cross and was one of the builders of the Community Development Committee, along with the late Clarence Bain.

Dr. Joyous Pickstock

Pickstock is known as the first Bahamian woman dentist to work for the Bahamian Government in the Ministry of Health. In 1986 Pickstock graduated from Meharry Medical College, Nashville, Tennessee, USA. In 1994 she received a Master's Degree in Dental Public Health from the University of London.

Pickstock is the former President of the Bahamas Dental Association and served as President of the Caribbean Atlantic Regional Association of Dentists. Pickstock also served as Executive Secretary (Bahamas) to the International Dental Federation (FDI). She is a member of the American Dental Association and the Academy of General Dentistry. She is a

(continued on page 53)

former Associate Professor in Dental Assisting at Success Training College, Nassau Bahamas. Pickstock has been employed with the Bahamas Ministry of Health for more than fourteen years. Pickstock now enjoys a limited private practice at Faith Dental Centre where she is Director.

Dr. Madlene Sawyer

Sawyer is known as the first Bahamian woman to specialize in Obstetrics and Gynecology. She is also the first Bahamian Gynecologist to sub-specialize in Perinatology and Endoscopic Surgery.

In 1989 Sawyer became a Consultant in Ob/GYN at the Rand Memorial Hospital in Freeport, GrandBahama. Sawyer was the chairperson of the Department of Ob/Gyn at Doctors Hospital.

Sawyer has delivered hundreds of babies in the country; unfortunately, a significant number of the mothers are teenagers who wished they had taken a better route in life. Dr. Sawyer's insatiable thirst to make a change in the lives of these women

(continued on page 55)

established the organization I AM S.M.A.R.T, BAHAMAS CHAPTER. S.M.A.R.T. is the acronym for Starting Mother (or Father) hood At the Right Time.

Dr. Sandra Dean-Patterson

Dean-Patterson is well known as the first Bahamian woman to establish the Bahamas Council for the Disabled in 1973. In 1997 Dean-Pattern received The Bahamas Order of Merit from the Bahamian Government. She also established Planned Parenthood in 1978 and in 1982 opened the Women's Crisis Centre, the first and oldest centre of its kind in the Caribbean. Dean-Patterson has lobbied to amend the 1991 Sexual Offences Act to include protection against battery for non-married couples.

Dean-Patterson also holds the title of the first woman president of The Bahamas Mental Health Association. Patterson is president and founder of The Bahamas Association of Social Workers.

(continued on page 57)

Dean-Patterson is an author who has written numerous publications such as: _Drug Abuse in Schools_, _Drug Abuse in Boys and Girls Industrial Schools_, _Alcohol Use and Abuse in the Bahamas_, and _Cocaine and the Bahamian Woman-Treatment Issues_. Her latest book is _Bahamian Women, Aids and Substance Abuse_.

Deanne Hanna-Ewers

CHAPTER 7
MUSIC

Maureen Duvalier

Maureen Duvalier is known as the first Bahamian female dancer to perform in The Bahamas World renowned Junkanoo parades. This pioneer Bahamian Junkanoo Queen was also a co-leader of the Mexicans Junkanoo Group in the 1950's. In addition to her role as a Junkanoo group leader, she is also the first woman to bring other female dancers to Nassau's Bay Street for Junkanoo and was the first female member of the Bahamas Musicians and Entertainers Union.

During the country's 30th year Independence Day celebration, the first annual Junkanoo Achievement Award was given to Duvalier to honor her for her historical contributions

(continued on page 60)

to Junkanoo. "I went on Bay Street as a little girl with my uncle Freddie Bowleg...everyone thought I was a boy. When I finally unmasked, [and they saw that I was a girl that was when] women started rushing."

Duvalier who is a multi-talented entertainer, became a professional vocalist at 17 years old with the world famous Freddie Munnings' Orchestra at the Silver Slippers.

Maureen was one of the few Bahamians to complete matriculation at Western Senior School at age 11. Maureen went on to attend New York University where she majored in drama from 1952-54; however, due to her Mother's illness, she returned home and did not complete her education.

One who loves Bahamian culture, Maureen was a pace-setter for women in Juankanoo. 'Ask Me Why I Run' is the hit on the only album Duvalier recorded in 1955.

Maureen is the first cousin of the late Haitian president Francoise 'Papa Doc' Duvalier. She was born in Nassau at Burial Ground Corner on East Street. Her father was born on Inagua Island along with two of his brothers and a sister, while his other four siblings were born in Haiti.

Antoinette Douglas

I n 1984, Antoinette Douglas, **WPC 1028,** played her way into the history books by becoming the first Bahamian woman to join the Royal Bahamas Police Force Band. Douglas played the flute in the world famous Royal Bahamas Police Force Band. Later, other women joined the Band. **WPC 1717** Lewis Bain, the first woman clarinet player; **WPC 1388** Gardiner, first woman Corporal in the Band; **WPC 1779** Butterfield, first female trumpet player; and **W/Cpl. 1723** Ferguson (Criminal Investigations Department) first woman alto saxophonist and steel pan player.

Later, there were other women added to this list such as; **WPC 350** Miller, first woman trombone player, and **Constable 142** Seymour became the first woman Reservist to play in the band.

Deanne Hanna-Ewers

CHAPTER 8
POLITICS

The Honorable Janet Gwennett Bostwick

Bostwick is widely known as the first Bahamian woman elected to the House of Assembly in 1982, and she remained in the House until she was defeated in the May 2, 2002 General elections. During her time in the House, Bostwick became the first woman to be appointed to the Cabinet, and the first woman to serve as Minister of Justice and Immigration. She was Minister of Foreign Affairs in 1994. She is also the first woman to serve as Attorney General. Her portfolio included Women's Affairs as one of the responsibilities. From September 1993 to November 1994,

(continued on page 64)

Bostwick served as Minister of Justice and Immigration. She has also on occasion acted as Prime Minister of the Commonwealth of The Bahamas. From 1992-1993, Bostwick served as Minister of Social Services, Housing and National Insurance.

Locally, Mrs. Bostwick served as President of the Free National Movement Women's Association. Boswick has also helped with the adoption of legislation geared towards improving the status of Bahamian Women. These legislation's include: The Matrimonial Causes Act (1978); The Bahamas Bar Act (1981); the Female Employee (Grant of Maternity Leave) Act (1981) and the Sexual Offences and Domestic Violence Act (1991). An attorney by profession, Bostwick served as President of the Bahamas Bar Association from 1980-82, and as Acting Magistrate in 1981.

Internationally, Bostwick has served as Vice President of the 51st Session of the United Nations General Assembly, where

(continued on page 65)

she chaired a plenary session of the Assembly. She has also served as President of the Caribbean Women for Democracy. Bostwick also was a representative on the Executive Committee of the Organization of the American States' Inter-American Commission on the Status of Women', and regional Vice chair of the Bureau of the United Nations Fourth World Conference on Women. During the conference held in Beijing in 1995, Bostwick also served as Coordinator for the Caribbean Region.

Ruby Ann Cooper Darling

In 1962, Ruby Ann Darling made history by becoming the first Bahamian woman to register to vote. Years later, Darling ran for Parliament on the Progressive Liberal Party's ticket. After her victory, she became the first Bahamian woman elected to the Bahamas Parliament on the PLP's ticket, and the second Bahamian woman to sit in parliament.

Later, in 1982, Darling was appointed to the Senate and in 1987 she was appointed a parliamentary Secretary with responsibility to the Prime Minister for Lodges and Fraternal Organizations. Darling now serves as a minister of the gospel in a local Baptist church.

Dame Dr. Doris L. Johnson, DBE (deceased)

J ohnson was the first Bahamian woman to run for a political party. She ran as a candidate for the Progressive Liberal Party, but was defeated. However from 1968 to 1969, Johnson became the first Bahamian woman to be appointed to the Cabinet (without portfolio). Later, she became the first Bahamian woman leader for the Government in the Senate, and was then appointed the first woman Minister of Transportation in 1979. Furthermore, in 1979, Johnson was the first Bahamian woman to Act as Governor General of the Bahamas. In that same year, Her Majesty the Queen made her a Dame Commander of the Most Excellent Order of the British Empire.

(continued on page 68)

Dame Doris Johnson was most known for her contributions to The Women's Suffragette. She was the author of several books; *The Quiet Revolution 1972*; *The Man on the Black Horse* a book written in dedication to the Independence of the Bahamas. She was also the author of the *Age of Awareness* written in 1973.

Rome Italia Johnson

J ohnson is well known as the first Bahamian woman to serve as Speaker of the House of Assembly, when she was unanimously elected to this position for the Commonwealth of the Bahamas on April 9, 1997. Johnson was the first woman elected to this post within the two hundred and sixty-eight year run of the parliament.

In 1997, she was elected Member of Parliament for the Garden Hills Constituency for the Free National Movement party. However, it was in 1992, that Johnson was first elected Member of Parliament for the St. Barnabas constituency, and served as Deputy Speaker of the House of Assembly. Johnson is an Insurance Executive and is a member of a Baptist Church.

Mary Naomi Mason-Ingraham
(deceased)

Ingraham made history as the founder and president of the Women's Suffrage Movement in the Bahamas. In 1951, this movement began asking for the petition for women's voting privileges and it ended in 1962 when women were granted the right to vote. Ingraham was the first to start this petition that secured some 550 signatures. This petition was then presented by C.R. Walker to the House of Assembly but it was denied.

In 1959, Ingraham and four other ladies read their petition to a visiting Colonial Secretary who encouraged them to solicit more signatures. Gerald Cash (a former Governor General)

(continued on page 71)

presented the second opportunity for their petition to be read in Parliament. Once again, it was denied, but House Members agreed to adjourn and hear the petition in the magistrate's court.

A year later, in 1960, the House of Assembly approved the right for women to vote. Thanks to the outstanding efforts of Ingraham, Bahamian women were able to vote for the very first time in the 1962 general elections.

Dr. Cynthia "Mother" Pratt, M.P., J.P.

I n 2002, Pratt was elected for a second term as Member of Parliament for the St. Cecilia constituency in New Providence, and it was in this same year that she made history by becoming the first Bahamian woman Deputy Prime Minister of the Commonwealth of The Bahamas, under the Progressive Liberal Party. Pratt was first elected into parliament in 1997.

Pratt has served the Bahamas Government for more than 34 years as a teacher. She served as a Head of Department at C.C. Sweeting Secondary High School and later as a Lecturer at the College of the Bahamas. She also served as Assistant Director

(continued on page 73)

of Student Activities at the College of the Bahamas. However, Pratt first began her career as a nurse.

Pratt is a Justice of the Peace for the Commonwealth of the Bahamas. She is the founder of the Coconut Grove Community Club for (males) and the St. Cecilia Community Club (for females) and a founding member of the Committee for a Better Bahamas.

Pratt, a sport enthusiast has several events named in her honor, which includes; The "Mother Pratt" Foundation, the "Mother Pratt" Basketball Classic and the "Mother Pratt" Annual Fun/Run/Walk, which is sponsored by the College of the Bahamas. Pratt has now retired from front line politics and is an ordained minister in a local church.

Georgianna Kathleen Symonette
(deceased)

S ymonette was known as the founder of the Progressive Liberal Party Women's Branch where she served as President. Recognizing the importance of women's vote, Symonette along with other ladies toured the Bahamas in order to obtain some 3,000 signatures to support women's right to vote. Symonette along with Mable Walker, Eugenia Lockhart, Mary Naomi Mason-Ingraham and others picketed the House of Assembly so that law makers may hear their cause. In 1962 the hard work and motivation of these determined women helped win the Bahamian women the right to vote.

The Honorable Loretta Butler-Turner

Butler-Turner is known as the first Bahamian woman to receive a Bachelor of Science degree in Mortuary Science from New England Institute, Boston Massachusetts where she graduated Summa Cum Laude with a degree in Embalmer and Business Administration.

In 2002 Butler-Turner was a candidate for the FNM in the St. Margaret constituency. Butler-Turner is a member of the Women's Association for the Free National Movement and holds the position of an executive member in the party and a past Deputy Chairman of the party. In the 2012 elections, Butler-Turner was voted in as the Member of Parliament for Long

(continued on page 76)

Island, Bahamas. She also holds the office of Deputy Prime Minister for the Free National Moment (The Opposition Party).

Butler-Turner is the granddaughter of the first Bahamian Governor General Sir Milo Butler and Lady Butler. Butler-Turner is a funeral director, who received her primary and secondary education from St. Andrews College, Nassau, Bahamas.

CHAPTER 9
RELIGION

Kenris L. Carey

C arey is known as the first Bahamian woman president of the Bahamas Methodist Group of Churches. Carey first joined Wesley Methodist Church and then went on to become the first youth leader at St. Michael's Methodist Church when it was founded.

Carey served as a speaker in the local Nassau Methodist circuit. In 1981 she became the Secretary for the World Methodist Council for the Caribbean Region, and five years later in 1986 she was elected Vice President of World Evangelism for the World of Methodist Council. Carey has also served in the following capacities: Chairperson–Evangelism

(continued on page 78)

for the Methodist Conference and Vice-President–
Foundation Conference.

Ella Lewis-Coulibaly

Coulibaly is the first Bahamian woman to receive a Masters Degree in Theology within the Catholic diocese. A devout Catholic, Coulibaly studied at Bethune Cookman College where she received her undergraduate degree in English Language and Journalism. During the summer of 1990 Coulibaly went on to study at St. John's University in Collegeville, Minnesota and then transferred to St. Meinrad School of Theology in St. Meinrad, Indiana where she graduated in 1995 with a degree in theology.

For more than ten years, Coulibaly held the position of director of the Christian Confederation Doctrine (CCD) a program for the Our Lady's Church. She is the former Coordinator of the Urban Renewal for the island of New Providence. The Urban renewal is an after school program to help students increase academic skills and artistic abilities.

Angela Palacious

On May 31, 2000, Palacious made history by becoming the first Bahamian woman to be ordained into the Anglican ministry during the 300 year-history of the Diocese of Nassau, which includes the Turks and Caicos Islands. Palacious was ordained by the late Rev Drexel Gomez at Christ Church Cathedral.

Palacious served as Coordinator, of the Diocese from 1999-2000. In addition, Palacious serves as Assistant Curate, at St. Margaret's Parish. She is the wife of Reverend Father James Palacious and continues to be a coveted speaker at numerous events. She is actively involved in the life of the Anglican Diocese of the Bahamas and the Turks and Caicos Islands.

Rev. Dr. Lavania Stewart *(deceased)*

R ev. Stewart was known as the first Bahamian woman Pastor in the Baptist church. Stewart worked in the Salem Mission Baptist Church with her husband for many years before his demise. In 1995 she dedicated The New Mt. Zion Missionary Baptist Church where she served as Pastor. The Rev. Dr. Lavania Stewart passed away New Years Eve 2008. Stewart was also a Justice of the Peace and a retired Librarian.

Dr. Susan Wallace

Wallace became the first Bahamian woman to earn a Doctorate degree in Christian Counseling. Wallace was responsible for establishing the first chapter of Women's Aglow in The Bahamas. Women's Aglow is an international Christian organization that helps improve women through education and training. Under her leadership as Regional Chairman of the Caribbean for Women's Aglow International, the number of chapters in the Caribbean grew from eight to 62.

Wallace is also the author of the following books: _A Layman's Guide to Counseling and Removing the Sackcloth_. She is also a poet and has written _Bahamian Scene_, 1970; _Island Echoe_s, 1973; and _Back Home_ 1975.

CHAPTER 10
SPORTS

Tonique Williams-Darling

Tonique Williams-Darling is the first Bahamian woman to secure an Olympic gold medal in an individual race. In the 2004 Summer Olympics held in Athens Greece, Williams-Darling won the gold medal in the 400m in the time of 49.07 seconds. After the Olympics, Williams-Darling won the overall Golden League-jackpot, cashing in $5000,000 after splitting the $1 million prize with Christian Olsson of Sweden. Williams-Darling also won a bronze medal at the 2004 IAAF World Indoor Championship in Budapest, Hungary. She beat Mexican world champion, Ana Guevara, breaking her 23 race-winning streak in the 400 meter race.

(continued on page 84)

The following year, Williams-Darling won the gold medal in the 400 meters at the 2005 World Championship in Athletics. At the 2006 Commonwealth Games, she won the silver medal in the 400m. Then, in 2009, she was inducted in her school's Athletic Hall of Fame.

Williams-Darling graduated from the University of South Carolina in 1999 with a Bachelor's degree. While in college, she won the US collegiate South Eastern Conference (SEC) 400-metre title in 1997. Williams-Darling is known as the fastest Caribbean woman ever for the 400 meters, clocking in at 49.07 seconds. Furthermore, because her accomplishments, the Independence Highway in Nassau, NP Bahamas was renamed in her honor, Tonique Williams-Darling Highway by the Bahamas Government in 2005. Williams-Darling is married to track and field athlete Dennis Darling.

Anita Doherty

Doherty is known as the first Bahamian woman to teach physical education in Grand Bahama. In 1972, she became the first Bahamian woman tennis player to win a triple crown in singles, doubles and mixed doubles matches within the same year. Doherty was also the first Bahamian woman to serve as President of the Grand Bahama Tennis and Squash Club. In addition, she also served as President of the Grand Bahama Amateur Athletic Association.

In 1977, Doherty was elected President of The Bahamas Netball Association where she spearheaded the organization of the first Caribbean Netball Tournament held in Nassau, New Providence.

Laverne Eve

In 1988 Eve made history by becoming the first Bahamian woman to compete in the Olympics Games, and then again in 1996. Eve competes in the javelin and the shot putt events. Eve is known as the "strong woman", who won the bronze medal in the Shot Put at the 1993 Central American and Caribbean Games. In 1998, Eve placed third at the Carifta Games in Maracaibo, Venezuela. In 2001, she placed first at the CAC Games in Guatemala City. In 2002, she placed first at the Commonwealth Games in Manchester and in that same year she placed 8th in Paris at the World Championship. In 2003, she placed first at the CAC Games in St. Georges, and second at the Pan Am Games in Santo Domingo. In 2004, Eve placed sixth

(continued on page 87)

in the Olympic finals in Athens. (Steven Downes for the IAAF August 2007).

Eve holds the Bahamas national discus record of 52.52m and hammer throw of 54.90m. At the age of 40 Eve secured the Bahamas' first medal at the Commonwealth Games with a throw of 60.54m in the javelin competition (Freeport News).

Eve's World Championship career began 25 years ago in Rome. Eve, now 47 years old at the time of this publication is still competing, "I keep going because I can. As long as I am healthy and I can throw, I don't see why I should not carry on." Eve received her degree from Louisiana State University and works for the Bahamas Ministry of Youth, Sports & Culture.

Debbie Ferguson-Mckenzie

Ferguson was one of the first Bahamian women to win a gold medal at the 2001 Olympic Games, in Sidney, Australia. Ferguson was also a member of the winning team for the 4x100m women's relay at the World Games held in Spain, August 1999. In 1996, She was also a part of the relay team that won the silver medal in the Olympic Games held in Atlanta, Georgia. In 1990 Ferguson was a part of the 400-metre relay team at the IAAF World Track and Field Championships in Seville, Spain.

Furthermore, Ferguson is the national record holder for The Bahamas in the 200m; she won this event at the 1999 Pan Am Games. She placed fifth at the World Games in Spain in 1999

(continued on page 89)

and won the same event at the ISTAF Grand Prix in Berlin that same year. In 1998, the Bahamian government awarded Ferguson with a Silver Jubilee Award for Athletics.

Ferguson, a former student of St. Andrew's School also graduated from the University of Georgia with honors.

Sevatheda Fynes

F ynes is one of the first Bahamian women to win a gold medal at the 2001 Olympic Games in Sidney, Australia. Fynes was also a part of the 1999 gold medal 400-meter relay team at the IAAF World Track and Field Championship in Seville, Spain. In 1998 Fynes won a silver medal in Beijing, China. She was also a member of the Bahamas' relay team that received a silver medal at the 1996 Olympic Games in Atlanta, Georgia.

While in College, Fynes became the first Bahamian woman to win two events in the National Collegiate Athletics Association (NCAA) Division I Championships. In 1992, Fynes won a silver medal in the 100m and in that same year she won

(continued on page 91)

a gold medal in the 200m race at the Carifta Games. At the 1993 Pan Am Junior Games she won silver medals in 100m and 200m races. In 1999 Fynes was listed as one of the five fastest women in the world. The Bahamian Government awarded Fynes the Sliver Jubilee Award for Athletics in 1998.

Fynes completed her high school education at C. R. Walker Secondary School. She earned an athletic scholarship to Southern University in New Orleans, Louisiana, but later transferred to Eastern Michigan University and then to Michigan State University where she received a degree in 1997. Earlier in her career (1985) Fynes was named Most Outstanding Athlete at the National Primary Schools Track and Field Championships in Nassau, NP Bahamas.

Eldece Clarke-Lewis

C larke-Lewis made history as part of the 4x100m Olympic team which won a gold medal for the Bahamas in the 2001 Olympic Games in Sidney, Australia. Lewis was also a part of the 1999 4x100-meter women's relay team that won the gold medal at the IAAF World Track and Field Championship in Seville, Spain. In 1996, Lewis won a sliver medal at the Olympic Games in Atlanta, Georgia.

In 1995 Lewis set a national record of 44.01 when she ran her leg in the 4x400-meter relay in Barrientos Memorial race in Cuba. In 1998, the Bahamian Government awarded Lewis the Silver Jubilee Awards for Athletics. Apart from her athletic achievements, Clarke-Lewis received a BA in Psychology and Sociology from Hampton University, Virginia.

Chandra Sturrup

Sturrup was among the first Bahamian women to win a gold medal at the 2001 Olympics Games held in Sidney, Australia. Sturrup was a member of the Bahamian women 4x100m-relay team that took the silver medal in the 1996 Olympic Games held in Atlanta, Georgia.

Sturrup won the gold medal in the 400-meter relay at the IAAF World Track and Field Championships in Seville, Spain. Sturrup is the Bahamas 100m dash record holder in the time of 10.95 seconds; she won the 100m event at the 1999 Pan Am Games held in Winnipeg, Canada with a time of 11.10 seconds.

Sturrup is the 1998 Commonwealth Games 100m Champion; and was named Bahamian Athlete of the Year in

(continued on page 94)

1997. In that same year Sturrup won a silver medal at the World Indoor Championships in Paris, France.

In 1995, Sturrup was the NCAA Division II Athlete of the year and the NCAA and CIAA outdoor and indoor champion. In 1998 Sturrup received the Silver Jubilee Medal for Athletics from the Bahamian government. Sturrup is a graduate of R. M. Bailey Senior High school and holds a Bachelors' degree in Business from Norfolk State University. Sturrup is still regarded as one of the fastest female starters in the world. Other worthy performances for Sturrup are achieving the bronze medal twice at the World Outdoors Meet in Edmonton, Canada in 2001 and in Saint-Denis, Paris in 2003 respectively.

OTHER NOTABLE WOMEN IN BAHAMIAN HISTORY

Dr. Vernell Allen: First Female Chief Medical Officer

Marsha Chriswell: First woman Pilot

Patricia Cozzi Cole: First Female Lawyer

Lynn Holowesko: First woman Ambassador to the Environment

Dame Bertha Isaacs: First woman to compete in International Tennis Tournament

Lady Patricia Isaacs: First woman Deputy to the Governor General

Alice Hill Jones: First woman Welfare Nurse

June Maura: First woman President of the Historical Society

Barbara Pierre: First woman Director of Immigration

(continued on page 96)

Dorothy Panza: First woman anchor on ZNS
television and radio stations

Juanita Colebrooke: First woman Chief of
Superintendent of Police

Myrtle Mott-Jones: First woman officer to work in the
Forensic Lab on The Royal
Bahamas Police Force.

Pauline Davis-Thompson

P auline Davis-Thompson is known as one of the first Bahamian women to win a gold medal in the 4x100m relay at the 2000 Summer Olympic Games held in Sydney, Australia. She originally finished in second place in the women's 200m behind Marion Jones, then in October 2007 Jones admitted taking performance enhancing drugs and was stripped of the title. On December 9, 2009, Davis-Thompson was finally awarded the gold medal.

In the 1996 Atlanta Olympics she narrowly missed out on a medal in the 400m. However, she helped the Bahamian team to win a silver medal in the 4X100 meter relay. She received her first World Championship gold medal two years later, in 1999, helping the Bahamian relay team to a victory.

(continued on page 98)

Her first high profile success came in 1995 where she won the silver medal in the 200 meters at the IAAF World Indoor Championships and won another silver medal in the 400 meters at the 1995 World Championship in Athletics.

The Bahamas' former national record-holder in the 400 meters, Davis-Thompson ran collegiately at Alabama. She graduated in 1989 with a B.A. in Communications and a minor in English. The Crimson Tide standout won the NCAA Indoor 200m dash in 1988 and took the NCAA Outdoor 400m crown in 1989, setting a collegiate record of 50.18 seconds.

On the Southeastern Conference (SEC) level, Davis-Thompson was a multiple champion, winning outdoor crowns in the 100m from 1986 to 1988. She also claimed indoor titles in the 55m and 200m in 1988. She raced to Southeastern Conference (SEC) Outdoor 4X100m relay titles in 1986 and 1987 and hoisted the Southeastern Conference (SEC) outdoor team trophy in 1986. Later, in 2005, she was recognized in the

(continued on page 99)

Southeastern Conference (SEC) Greats Program, which was designed to honor those who helped establish the rich athletic tradition in the conference.

The five-time Olympian and seven-time World Championship competitor retired after her career-topping effort in the 4X100 meter race in 2000, but not before achieving status as a heroine in her country. Because of her performance with the Bahamian 4X100m relay team that earned a silver medal at the 1996 Olympic in Atlanta, Davis-Thompson and the group of young ladies became known as "The Golden Girls." These ladies were honored with a mural bearing their images that greet visitors at the Nassau International Airport. A postage stamp was also issued in their honor in 1998, and the Governor-General of the Bahamas presented "The Golden Girls" with a silver Jubilee Award for their contributions to athletics.

In 2007, Pauline Davis-Thompson spent the year serving as a volunteer coach. The, after a stint as the founder and coach

(continued on page 100)

of PDT International Track Club, where she trained elite-level post collegiate athletes such as; two-time Olympic gold medalist Monique Hennagan of the U.S., Olympian Christine Amertil, Addis Huyler of the Bahamas and Pete-Gaye Dowdie of Jamaica she became a full-time track and field coach on J.J. Clark's staff in Tennessee where she presently works with the women's sprints/jumps & hurdles group. In addition, since 1989 she has served as District Marketing Manager of sports/tourism for the Bahamas Ministry of Tourism in Atlanta, GA. Furthermore, Davis-Thompson has also held two key track and field governance positions since 2003, underscoring the high regard given to her from those in the sport. Globally, she has served as a women's committee member for the International Association of Athletics Federations (IAAF), an organization responsible for establishing policies and procedures for promoting women in track and field throughout the world. For her home country, she has filled a role as

(continued on page 101)

Bahamas Association of Athletic Associations (BAAA) International coordinator. In this role, she serves as a liaison between the BAAA's Federation and overseas-based athletes. Davis-Thompson is married to Jamaican Olympian Mark Thompson.

Deanne Hanna-Ewers

ABOUT THE AUTHOR

V. Deanne Hanna-Ewers

V Deanne Hanna-Ewers is the sixth of eight children born to Mr. Cyril and Leanczar Hanna. She grew up in the neighborhood of Penny Saving Subdivision located off Soldier Road West. She is an educator by profession, a singer, songwriter and an administrator. She presently reside in West Palm Beach, Florida with her husband and two kids.

As a child, Deanne always enjoyed reading and writing. Her dad would come home and rest the current newspaper in a rocking chair and she would pick it up and read it. After noticing her interest in reading the newspaper, he would later begin to give her the newspapers and she would read the headlines each day.

One day while reading the newspapers she read about the first Bahamian woman to work as a pilot for Bahamasair. She also read about

(continued on page 104)

the first Bahamian woman to play in The Royal Bahamas Police Band. These two articles ignited a flame in her heart to do something significant as a woman. Her accomplishments to date have not gotten her on this distinguished list, but fate would have it that she would write about these high achievers who have set high standards for women in the Bahamas, as well as the Caribbean. Deanne considers herself honored to have written this book and hopes that you would consider yourself privileged to read it.